1   Introduction

In recent years, two types of behavior by branded gasoline marketers have come under antitrust scrutiny: zone pricing for wholesale sale of gasoline to retail stations and territorial restraints on independent distributors (jobbers) that deliver gasoline to other retail stations. These territorial restraints are called "redlining" by opponents of the practice. Commentators have suggested that zone pricing and territorial restraints lead to higher retail prices for gasoline. Regarding redlining, the Petroleum Marketers Association of America (2003) wrote that the "obvious effect of redlining is to reduce the number of competitors and, hence, the level of competition.... [R]efiners are afforded a monopoly on the brand..." The Federal Trade Commission (FTC) has investigated the effects of these practices at least twice, in the 1998-2001 Western States Gasoline Pricing investigation and in the 1998-99 investigation of the Exxon/Mobil merger.[1] Although the Commission concluded that these practices could not be challenged as a matter of law given the facts in those specific cases, some people remain concerned that both practices can reduce consumer welfare, particularly in concentrated markets with entry impediments. Several states are considering legislation to ban the use of price zones or redlining.

As a general matter, assessing whether a practice is likely to reduce consumer welfare involves several steps. First, is there a sound economic theory that explains how the practice could result in consumer harm? Second, what are the conditions necessary for such harm to occur? Third, what is the evidence whether such conditions are met with regard to the industry and practice at issue? Fourth, are there procompetitive (or competitively benign) reasons for

---

[1] Western States Gasoline Pricing, FTC File No. 981-0187, available at http://www.ftc.gov/os/caselist/9810187.htm, and Exxon Corporation and Mobil Corporation, FTC File No. 991-0077, Docket No. C-3907, available at http://www.ftc.gov/os/caselist/c3907.htm.

these practices? The existence of the latter can be inferred if the practices are common even in circumstances where the conditions for competitive harm are not present. Where the practice lacks a solid theory of anticompetitive effects or lacks evidence supporting the theory, the practice is unlikely to lead to competitive harm even without strong evidence supporting the procompetitive explanations for the practice. Conversely, in situations with a solid anticompetitive effects theory and evidence that is consistent with the theory (and inconsistent with alternative explanations), the practice is likely to lead to competitive harm unless substantial evidence supports efficiency justifications and evidence indicates that the likely procompetitive benefits of the practice outweigh the likely anticompetitive harm.

This paper reviews the economic theories of anticompetitive harm that could arise from price zones and redlining, as well as several procompetitive explanations for the practices. We begin with a brief review of types of gasoline distribution and define the two marketing practices in Section 2. In Section 3 we review the literature on vertical restraints in gasoline marketing. Section 4 considers both anticompetitive and procompetitive explanations for price zones, as well as the evidence available on each explanation, and Section 5 does the same for redlining. Section 6 concludes.

2   Gasoline Marketing Background

2.1 Types of Gasoline Distribution

Most branded gasoline retailers fall into one of three basic types: company operated stations, lessee dealers, and open dealers.[2] Company operated stations are owned and operated by the wholesale marketer. Lessee dealer stations are owned by the marketer, which leases them to independent businesspeople to operate. Open dealers own and operate their own stations, and

_____

[2] For a more detailed discussion of the types of gasoline stations, see Shepard (1993) and Kleit (2003).

3

contract with a marketer, or more likely a jobber acting as an agent for the marketer, to use the marketer's brand.[3]

The two basic types of distribution are direct supply and jobber supply. Company operated stations and lessee dealers are typically supplied directly by the marketer, while open dealers are typically supplied by jobbers who buy gasoline from the marketer at a terminal. Lessee dealers typically pay a delivered price, often referred to as the dealer tank wagon (DTW) price. Jobbers pay a posted price at the terminal,[4] often referred to as the rack price, and then set delivered wholesale prices to the open dealers they supply as well as the jobbers' lessee dealers. In the United States, the breakdown of gasoline volumes sold through different station types is roughly 19% company operated, 20% DTW (lessee dealer and potentially some open dealers that are direct supplied), and 61% jobber supplied.[5] Areas that contain both direct-supplied and jobber-supplied stations of the same brand are referred to as dual distribution areas. Dual distribution areas could arise as a result of mergers, for example, where historically one of the merging marketers used jobbers in a particular area while the other supplied its stations directly. Also, market growth may have allowed jobber-supplied and direct-supplied areas to grow near one another. Redlining issues tend to arise most often in dual distribution areas.

In many ways, lessee dealer stations are very similar to company operated stations. Marketers, by setting the rent, setting the DTW price, and specifying minimum standards of

---

[3] Jobbers own and operate some of the stations that they supply, and may also own stations that they lease to dealers. Jobbers often represent more than one brand of gasoline, and often own or lease multiple stations. On occasion, jobbers also use price zones. See Maryland Energy Administration (2001). Although a jobber has the same incentives to use price zones as marketers, a jobber may lack the ability to enforce zones unless the jobber leases stations it owns, in which case the jobber, like the branded marketer, can prevent its lessee dealers from switching suppliers.

[4] Some jobbers will also negotiate discounts off the branded rack price.

[5] Energy Information Administration (EIA), Petroleum Marketing Monthly, Table 7. These figures include both branded and unbranded gasoline sales.

4

station operation, have a significant influence on a lessee dealer's station. While the marketer is not able to ensure effort levels or set the retail price for these stations, the marketer can address these problems to some degree through contractual terms, such as minimum volume requirements. One reason marketers choose to have lessee dealers rather than company operated stations is to deal with agency problems. If marketers have a difficult time monitoring the efforts of store managers, turning the store manager (who earns a salary) into a lessee dealer (who is the residual claimant on station profits) removes the monitoring problem. This is true because the lessee dealer's profits are tied to its performance in a way that marketers may not be able to replicate at the same cost with employee compensation.[6]

Another reason that marketers have lessee dealer stations is that many states have some form of divorcement law that bars marketers from owning and operating retail stations outright, or that limits the number of retail stations that the marketer may own and operate in an area. By building a large network of lessee dealers in these areas, branded marketers ensure a relatively steady retail outlet for their gasoline.[7] Jobbers and open dealers are not as reliable as a long-run outlet for a marketer's gasoline because jobbers and open dealers can and do switch brands.[8] The use of lessee dealers varies across geographic regions; for example, on the West Coast, DTW

---

[6] For example, a marketer may own a station with automobile service bays, and repeat business may depend substantially on the quality of service work the dealer performs. The marketer could, in theory, hire a station manager whose compensation depends on some measurement of the quality of work performed, or could periodically inspect the quality of work, but either of these solutions may be substantially more costly than simply leasing the station to an entrepreneurial dealer. See the discussion of Taylor (2000) in Section 3.

[7] In states without divorcement laws, the marketer can build a network of company operated stations to be a steady retail outlet for its gasoline, but will likely have some lessee dealers as well.

[8] Marketers' contracts with their open dealers and jobbers may create costs to switching brands. For example, a marketer may loan money to an open dealer to improve its station under favorable terms that are negated if the dealer switches brands. However, these switching costs are not able to tie the station to the marketer as tightly as owning the land and station and leasing these assets, because, among other reasons, dealers and jobbers who switch can "re-finance" a loan under a new contract with a new brand.

sales are nearly 50% of the total, while the comparable figure in the Midwest is below 10%.[9]

Because the decision to use a company-operated or lessee dealer station depends on a number of

factors, including whether the station has service bays or a convenience store (see Section 3), one

should not compare the fraction of company-operated stations across markets without controlling

for station characteristics. Without the security of a lessee dealer network that is contractually

obligated to buy the marketers' gasoline (or company-operated stores, where permitted), branded

marketers would likely be less willing to make the complementary investments to build a

branded presence in an area.

2.2 Price Zones

Gasoline marketers typically define a price zone as a contiguous set of gasoline stations

of the same brand that face a common set of competitive factors, including competing brands.

Within the zone, lessee dealer stations pay the same DTW price; the zone may also contain

company operated stations, but typically will not include jobber-supplied dealers. These zones

may change over time as station characteristics or the competitive factors facing the station

change. Price zones are not a new phenomenon,[10] but, over time, the price zones have generally

decreased in size as marketers have become more able to process pricing information at the

station level.

2.3 Redlining

Redlining refers mainly to the practice of marketers creating territories in which jobbers

are precluded from or limited in branding new stations, or supplying existing branded stations.

---

[9] EIA, Petroleum Marketing Monthly, Table 43.

[10] For example, ExxonMobil has used price zones "throughout the United States for more than 30 years." Statement of J.S. Carter, Regional Director, United States, ExxonMobil Fuels Marketing Company, in "Gas Prices: How are They Really Set?" Hearings Before the Permanent Subcommittee of Investigations of the Committee on Governmental Affairs, United States Senate, April 30 and May 2, 2002 ("Levin Hearings").

The FTC defined two types of redlining: "territorial, in which the contract between the refiner [branded marketer] and the jobber gives the refiner the right to refuse to approve the jobber's request to supply branded gasoline to independent stations or supply its own stations in specific price zones," and "site-specific, in which the contract includes financial disincentives for the jobber to sell in locations directly supplied by the refiner [branded marketer] and prevents a jobber from shipping low-priced gasoline to stations located in high-priced zones."[11] Section 5 discusses possible reasons for these restrictions.

3   Literature on Vertical Restraints in Gasoline Marketing

In general, the empirical economics literature on vertical restraints in gasoline marketing has shown that these restraints are procompetitive. These findings are consistent with the bulk of the theoretical literature on vertical restraints, which finds several procompetitive motivations for this behavior. For example, a manufacturer may try to affect downstream markups in order to expand the manufacturer's sales, induce resellers to maintain product quality or service levels, or align its interests with those of its resellers. To do so, the manufacturer may impose maximum markups (directly limiting resellers' abilities to increase margin), two-part tariffs (indirectly limiting markups through a fixed fee and a lower transfer price), exclusive territories (making resellers the residual claimants on local profits), or tying (monitoring the intensity of use of one product by observing the frequency of purchase of another product).[12] In this section, we review the relevant literature on vertical restraints in the gasoline industry.

---

[11] *See* "Statement of Commissioners Sheila F. Anthony, Orson Swindle, and Thomas B. Leary concerning Western States Gasoline Pricing Investigation, File No. 981-0187," available at http://www.ftc.gov/os/2001/05/wsgpiswindle.htm ("Western States Gasoline Statement").

[12] Viscusi *et al.* (1992), pp. 222-24, 234-48.

A number of states have divorcement regulations that limit the ability of gasoline marketers to own and operate their stations. Vita (2000) provides the most careful and comprehensive study of the effect of these regulations, and finds that retail gasoline prices average about two to three cents per gallon higher in states with divorcement laws than states without such laws, all else equal. His findings are consistent with those of earlier studies on divorcement. Barron and Umbeck (1984), who looked at the effects of Maryland's divorcement law, found that divorcement increased average full-service prices by 6.7 cents per gallon, and increased average self-service prices by about two cents per gallon.[13]

Other papers examine the ownership structure in gasoline marketing. Shepard (1993) looks at the effect of vertical integration on retail prices and station characteristics to test the hypothesis that vertical integration ameliorates both double marginalization and moral hazard issues. She finds that prices at company-owned stations are six cents per gallon lower than prices at jobber-supplied stations for full-service regular gasoline and ten cents per gallon lower for full-service premium gasoline, but differences in prices across other organizational structures, such as lessee dealer stations, for self-service gasoline are not statistically significant. Taylor (2000) uses a principal-agent framework to examine effects of monitoring conditions on the choice of vertical structure. Using data on California service stations, he concludes that the probability that a gasoline marketer will lease (rather than operate) a service station is much higher if the station has repair bays or full-service pumps than if the station does not have these features.[14] He suggests that this pattern reflects the fact that when a station has repair bays and

---

[13] Blass and Carlton (2001) estimate that divorcement increases costs of operation by about 3-4 cents per gallon.

[14] Taylor shows that stations with repair services are more than seven times more likely to be operated as lessee stations than company-operated stations, all else equal. Similarly, full-service stations are about five times more likely to be operated as lessee stations than company-operated stations.

full-service operations, it is more difficult for the marketer to monitor effort, thus favoring operation by a lessee (who becomes the residual claimant on profits) rather than by a salaried employee.

Two unpublished papers found that vertical integration between gasoline marketing and retailing can lead to higher prices, although problems with the papers limit their usefulness. Hastings (2002) examines the effect of ARCO's 1997 acquisition and rebranding of 260 Thrifty gasoline stations in southern California. About two-thirds of the rebranded stations became company-operated stations, while the remainder stayed dealer-operated as the result of prior contractual arrangements. Using this difference in the method of operating the stations, Hastings finds that rebranding the stations had a significant positive effect on prices, but the difference did not depend on whether ARCO operated or leased the stations. As the paper does not consider the value that consumers place on the ARCO brand,[15] one cannot use the paper to determine whether consumer welfare increased or decreased as a result of the acquisition. Hastings and Gilbert (2002) conduct an empirical examination of West Coast gasoline markets, and conclude that increasing vertical integration increases wholesale gasoline prices. However, because it focuses on *wholesale* price effects, the paper cannot resolve the issue of whether vertical integration increases *retail* prices.[16]

---

[15] Although gasoline must meet minimum standards regardless of brand, marketers attempt to create a perception of brand value for consumers in a variety of ways, including advertising the brand and the specific additives used in the brand's gasoline (such as Chevron's "Techron"), the appearance of the station, or conveniences (such as ExxonMobil's Speed Pass, which allows consumers to pay at the pump more quickly than a standard credit card transaction). The perception that a one brand of gasoline is of higher quality than another brand may allow the marketer to charge a higher price for the brand. This phenomenon is not limited to the gasoline market, but is common in consumer products; for example, national brands of grocery products generally command a price premium over store brands because of the perception of higher quality. In California, ARCO was considered a "discount" brand – unlike the major brands, such as Exxon, ARCO did not take credit cards – but ARCO commanded a price premium over lesser brands such as Thrifty.

[16] The paper has other methodological problems, such as the use of the unbranded wholesale price in an area (the West Coast) where unbranded sales are minimal; the fact that the merger in the study immediately followed

Opponents of price zones and redlining have proposed "open supply" laws that would prevent marketers from restricting where jobbers and dealers can sell and purchase gasoline.[17] Comanor and Riddle (2003) discuss one such proposed law in California, and argue that open supply laws would increase average branded retail prices by about two cents per gallon and average unbranded retail prices by four to six cents per gallon. About 80% of the stations would face higher prices under an open supply law as arbitrage shifts competition from localized retail markets to the broader wholesale market. Intuitively, dealers who, absent open supply laws, received a low DTW price because of particularly intense local competition would pay a higher price.[18] Similarly, Keeley and Elzinga (2003) conclude that the effect of open supply legislation would be to raise wholesale and retail prices by reducing the use of efficient methods of distribution and eliminating efficient price discrimination.[19]

Recent experimental work by Deck and Wilson (2003) that attempts to directly examine the effect of zones also shows that eliminating price zones is likely to have an adverse effect on retail prices and consumer welfare. Their experiment consists of four branded marketers and four retailers, each affiliated with one of the brands. Each retailer operates one isolated station and

---

California's switch to a unique, higher-cost gasoline specification, which increased the level and variance of West Coast gasoline prices; and the use of Phoenix as a control city in assessing the Tosco/Unocal merger even though supply and demand conditions in southern California directly affect gasoline prices in Phoenix, because much of the gasoline consumed in Phoenix arrives via pipeline from Los Angeles.

[17] These proposed laws would not prohibit price zones directly, but would allow both jobbers and lessee dealers to arbitrage across terminal racks, which would effectively eliminate a marketer's ability to use price zones. Any dealer in a high-priced zone (i.e., where the DTW price exceeds the rack price plus delivery price) would opt out of direct supply from the marketer. Of course, as discussed in the text, equilibrium rack prices would change in response to the imposition of an open supply law.

[18] For example, see Tirole (1997), pp. 137-40, on the welfare implications of price discrimination. In testimony before Congress, Professor Preston McAfee noted that "Elimination of price zones…will tend to increase prices in the most competitive and also the poorest areas. Zone pricing is essentially the same phenomenon as the senior citizen discount at the movie theater" and that such price discrimination benefits consumers. Levin Hearings, p. 117.

[19] Their model is similar to that of O'Brien and Shaffer (1994), in which nonlinear pricing in an intermediate goods market benefits consumers because a power buyer is able to negotiate a lower price to gain an advantage over rivals, which in turn lowers the final goods price.

one station in a centrally-located retail cluster. The authors examine how participants in the experiment set wholesale and retail prices under a regime when zone pricing – a separate wholesale price for the isolated station and the station in the retail cluster for each brand – is permitted and under a regime where the wholesale price must be the same for both stations of that brand. They illustrate the intuition behind the Comanor and Riddle and the Keeley and Elzinga results: marketers react to a ban on price zones by reducing wholesale prices in isolated areas, where retail competition is less intense, and increasing wholesale prices in the retail cluster, where competition is more intense. Retailers capture any locational rents in the isolated areas, so the pump prices in those areas remain roughly unchanged, while the pump price rises in the cluster, decreasing consumer welfare.[20] Deck and Wilson also provide results consistent with the empirical literature on vertical integration: pump prices are lower when marketers directly control retail prices because the marketers eliminate the double markup that exists with separate ownership of refining and retailing.

A related literature examines franchise agreements and, in particular, the motivation for vertical restrictions that franchisors impose on franchisees. Klein and Saft (1985) show that franchisors have an incentive to use tie-in sales as a low-cost mechanism to ensure franchisees maintain minimum quality levels.[21] The authors also show that franchisors can deter cheating on contract terms such as product quality or service level by renting rather than selling the franchise location. If franchisees invest enough sunk costs in developing the business and are able to earn

---

[20] The Deck and Wilson analysis abstracts from changes in lease terms. If marketers can fully capture any locational rents through increased monthly land rents, marketers can effectively mimic price zones. As Section 4.2 discusses, several reasons exist for why payments from dealers to marketers for the use of the land may not reflect the full value of the land and station.

[21] Klein and Saft also provide an example of a franchisor, Chicken Delight, that required franchisees to purchase paper supplies from the franchisor as a mechanism to monitor the proportion of high-margin sales (individual dinners) to low-margin sales (buckets of chicken) and to extract some of the surplus from franchise locations with a higher proportion of high-margin sales.

11

sufficient quasi-rents from the franchise operation, the threat of contract termination and the associated loss of the stream of quasi-rents may be sufficient to deter franchisees from cheating on the contract. Baskin-Robbins and McDonald's both use this technique.[22] Mathewson and Winter (1985) develop a model in which the franchisor has an incentive to set maximum prices and/or minimum store hours as a way of preventing franchisees from incorrectly claiming that a low-demand state of the world occurred, then pocketing the scarcity rents. As with the Klein and Saft paper, vertical restrictions in franchise contracts serve to reduce the likelihood of franchisee free-riding. Franchisors do not need market power to find these restrictions profitable to employ. Neither of these papers directly examines vertical restrictions in gasoline marketing and retailing, but the types of restrictions – including requirements to purchase gasoline from the marketer and the use of leases for retailers – are similar to those discussed in the franchising literature.

4   Price Zones

Much of the controversy around price zones seems to stem from the fact that the differences in DTW prices that marketers charge retailers may not be explained solely by differences in delivery costs, but may be based in part on local market conditions.[23] The Exxon/Mobil Analysis to Aid Public Comment states that "These DTW prices generally are unrelated to the cost of hauling fuel from the terminal to the retail store."[24] Critics of zone

---

[22] Klein and Saft, p. 352, fn. 24. Kaufmann and Lafontaine (1994) show that McDonald's leaves expected quasi-rents to franchisees on the order of $300,000 to $455,000 in 1982 dollars, although those authors attribute this finding to the desire of McDonald's to find franchisees whose livelihoods are tied to the success of their outlets, combined with wealth constraints on that type of individual. Dnes (1993) provides a survey of franchise restrictions in the UK.

[23] Levin Hearings, p. 9. One report noted that wholesale price differentials for nearby stations in one location were between seven and twelve cents per gallon, which is likely higher than differences in delivery costs. Levin Hearings, p. 91.

[24] Analysis to Aid Public Comment, Exxon Corporation and Mobil Corporation, FTC File No. 991-0077, Docket No. C-3907, available at http://www.ftc.gov/os/caselist/c3907.htm.

12

pricing further argue that the existence of wholesale price differences that are not based on differences in costs implies that wholesale markets for gasoline are not competitive. The argument is that zone pricing reflects price discrimination, that price discrimination requires market power, and that therefore branded marketers that use zone pricing are exercising market power, perhaps due to coordination. Indeed, the Commission viewed the presence of price zones as an indication of market power.[25]

Even if zone pricing reflects price discrimination and the existence of price discrimination reflects market power, it does not follow that zone pricing as a practice reduces consumer welfare. If zone pricing simply reflects the existence of market power (unilaterally or through coordination), removing zone pricing will not eradicate the market power unless zone pricing contributes to the ability to exercise market power. In addition, if zone pricing reflects price discrimination but does not otherwise make the exercise of market power more durable or effective (we discuss this possibility in the next two sections), the impact of zone pricing on consumer welfare is ambiguous. When sellers practice price discrimination, prices are lower to some consumers and higher to others than would be the case if sellers charged uniform prices. The net effect of price discrimination on consumers is therefore uncertain and overall welfare may increase to the extent output increases (Tirole (1997)). Thus, even if the existence of zone pricing reflected the existence of market power among wholesale marketers, the practice itself

---

[25] The Exxon/Mobil Analysis of Proposed Consent Order to Aid Public Comment (available at http://www.ftc.gov/os/1999/11/exxonmobilana.pdf) said that "The use of price zones indicates that these competitors set their prices on the basis of their competitors' prices, rather than on the basis of their own costs. This is an earmark of oligopolistic market behavior." See also Statement of Chairman Robert Pitofsky and Commissioners Sheila F. Anthony and Mozelle W. Thompson *in re* Exxon/Mobil (available at http://www.ftc/gov/os/1999/11/exxonmobilpitofskystatement.pdf): "[T]here was some evidence of coordinated action in parts of metropolitan areas (usually termed 'price zones')..." Commissioner Swindle, in a separate statement, argued that only in highly concentrated retail markets (which he defined as metropolitan areas) was the presence of price zones an important factor in determining whether removing a competitor would facilitate coordination. (http://www.ftc.gov/os/1999/11/exxonmobilswindle.pdf)

need not reduce consumer welfare. A justification to ban the practice on competition grounds must be based on a finding that zone pricing in some way contributes to the ability to exercise market power.

However, the question of whether the presence of zone pricing reflects market power is important in analyzing the nature of competition in the marketing segment of the petroleum industry, particularly in the context of a merger. If there is existing market power (particularly reflecting coordinated behavior) in a market, then a merger in that market is more likely to raise competitive concerns. As a starting point, even if zone pricing actually reflects price discrimination (that is, the differences in prices do not reflect differences in a true measure of costs, a concept that may be broader than just transport costs), this alone does not indicate the presence of market power because price discrimination is not a good indicator of the existence of substantial market power (Klein and Wiley (2003) and Baumol and Swanson (2003)).[26]

Thus, a key issue for merger analysis is whether certain features of gasoline marketing make the existence of zone pricing unlikely unless there is substantial market power. First, Keeley and Elzinga (2003) note that where entry and exit of retail stations are relatively easy, it would be difficult to maintain price differences that are not based on costs. Because price zones are used in all parts of the country,[27] including places where entry and exit are ongoing, differences in DTW prices may be closely related to differences in the cost of supplying stations. Such costs would include differences in the value of particular station locations that are not otherwise captured in lease terms. This and other reasons that differences in wholesale prices

---

[26] Both Klein and Wiley and Baumol and Swanson note that almost all firms possess some degree of economic market power, in the sense that a firm finds it profitable to charge a price above marginal cost; indeed, pricing above marginal cost is necessary to stay in business in markets with fixed costs. Most firms do not possess market power in the sense that antitrust practitioners typically use the term.

[27] "Redlining and price zones are nationwide practices." Western States Gasoline Statement, footnote 1.

14

may not be explained solely by differences in the marketer's cost of transporting gasoline to different stations are discussed further below.

In any event, retail price variation is not a sign of less-than-competitive wholesale markets. Consider what retail prices would look like if all stations were independently owned and operated and all paid a uniform wholesale price. These stations will still need to be profitable (that is, make at least zero economic profits) to stay in business over the longer run. Local supply and demand conditions will influence the prices at an individual station. The types of factors that will affect its demand include traffic flows, population density, and the amount of local retail competition, while the types of factors that will affect its supply include land cost, station format, labor costs, and taxes. Differences in local retail competition will arise even in competitive markets, because local competition will be affected by the number of stations that can operate profitably in an area as well as government zoning regulations.

For example, consider two areas with similar initial retail competition with similar prices but different land costs or real estate taxes. For a station to be profitable in the higher-cost area, it will need higher prices or volumes (or both). Over the long run, this will likely affect local competition by causing some stations in the higher-cost area to exit. An area may also be less competitive if demand increases but government zoning regulations do not allow new stations to enter. Over time, as demand at each station grows, the equilibrium price of gasoline will increase relative to what it would be in a growing area where new stations can enter easily. Where entry of new stations is constrained, the higher prices help relieve congestion at a station. When faced with higher prices where few stations are located, some consumers will buy gasoline elsewhere at lower prices, relieving the congestion.[28] If instead of each station being independently owned

---

[28] Congestion may occur only at peak demand hours.

and operated, marketers owned and operated all of their branded stations, the same factors would

create retail price variation. Retail prices would still depend on demand and cost conditions for

each station. Thus, retail price variation is to be anticipated, whether or not wholesale prices

vary. The question is whether wholesale price variation that follows to some extent the retail

price variation is a natural outgrowth of the nature of the market or reflects potential

anticompetitive behavior at the marketer level.

4.1 Anticompetitive Theories of Price Zones

The principal antitrust concerns relating to zone pricing appear to be that the practice may

allow marketers to coordinate prices more effectively and to deter entry through localized price

cuts.[29] For example, according to Vigdor (2003, p. 12), "Zone pricing apparently facilitated

oligopolistic pricing or non-cost-based pricing. Such pricing suggested to the Commission [in the

context of the Exxon/Mobil investigation] that the markets for gasoline were not performing

competitively." The FTC also noted entry-deterring effects of price zones in the context of the

Exxon/Mobil investigation, commenting that

> Market incumbents also use price zones to target entrants without having to lower price
> throughout a broader marketing area. With a large and dispersed network of stores, an
> incumbent can target an entrant by cutting price at a particular store, without cutting
> prices throughout a metropolitan area. By targeting price-cutting competitors, incumbents
> can (and have) deterred entrants from making significant investments in gasoline stations
> (which are specialized, sunk cost facilities) and thus from expanding to a scale at which
> the entrant could affect price throughout the broader metropolitan area.[30]

---

[29] Dealers also complain that price zones (along with the contractual requirement to purchase gasoline from the
marketer) are used to create an incentive for individual dealers to *reduce* retail prices if the marketer believes the
price is too high. Dealers have tried to increase prices above the levels suggested by branded marketers and, to
create an incentive for the dealers to reduce prices, the marketers may increase the DTW price in order to deprive
the dealers of the additional margin. (Levin Hearings, p. 9) As reductions in retail price generally benefit consumers,
we do not address this as a separate anticompetitive theory.

[30] Federal Trade Commission, "Analysis of Proposed Consent Order to Aid Public Comment in the Matter of Exxon
Corporation and Mobil Corporation, File No. 991 0077, Docket No. C-3907," available at
http://www.ftc.gov/os/1999/11/exxonmobilana.pdf. ("Exxon/Mobil Analysis to Aid Public Comment.")

4.1.1 More Effective Coordination Theory

The first theory we consider is whether zone pricing could make anticompetitive coordination among wholesale marketers more effective. Coordination among rivals requires that they are able to reach consensus, detect deviations from the coordinated outcome, and punish such deviations. Zone pricing could make coordination more likely if it made one of these prongs more readily accomplished while not making one of the other prongs more difficult. The theory that zone pricing could make coordination more likely is that retail gasoline prices are readily monitored, while wholesale prices are less transparent. Although rack prices are posted publicly, marketers can and do give discounts off the posted price; DTW prices are generally less visible to competitors than rack prices. If the use of price zones permitted marketers to track more accurately DTW prices through the observation of retail prices, price zones could facilitate tacit coordination over wholesale prices by making deviations from the coordinated outcome easier to detect. In addition, by making wholesale competition more localized, zone pricing could reduce the costs to marketers of punishing firms that undercut a collusive agreement.

In theory, zone pricing could make coordination easier. However, theory alone is not enough to condemn such practices as potentially anticompetitive – rather, it is necessary to assess whether the evidence supports a finding that such an outcome is likely. For instance, does the nature of zone pricing as it has evolved support a conclusion that detection of deviations from a coordinated outcome or punishment is easier? Does the existence of zone pricing impact the ability to reach consensus? As we describe below, the evidence appears to cut against the theory and suggests that, as a general matter, zone pricing is unlikely to make coordination more probable or more effective.

First, coordination over prices within zones likely requires coordination over the zones themselves. If two marketers do not know whether their stations are in the same price zone, neither marketer will know how to react to price cuts by the other. Is the competitor cheating, or is it reacting to competition from a station that it considers part of its price zone but that the other marketer considers too distant to be concerned about? The evidence suggests that different marketers often use price zones that are of significantly different shapes and sizes.[31]

Second, within a marketer's price zone, there can be significant retail price variation among its own branded stations. This variation would reduce the ability of marketers to infer the DTW prices of its competitors from observations of retail prices.[32, 33] Both of these factors suggest that zone pricing as it currently exists may not improve the ability to detect deviations.

Third, localized wholesale competition reduces the cost of punishing price-cutters only if such price cutting is also localized. But it is not clear that competitive responses can be limited

---

[31] Executives of five major oil companies responded to a question regarding what percentage of each company's zones include a single dealer. The answers ranged from "a very small percentage" (ChevronTexaco), "relatively small" (BP), and "less than 10 percent" (ExxonMobil) to "fifty-three percent" (Shell Oil) to "all single-dealer zones" (Marathon Ashland). See Levin Hearings, pp. 71-72. The Western States Gasoline Pricing investigation, concluded after the Exxon-Mobil investigation, "revealed no evidence of coordination by refiners in their use of price zones or in the zones' geographic locations or dimensions [in the Western states]." (Western States Gasoline Statement). From this we conclude that a typical price zone for Marketer A will include a station selling Marketer B's brand, but Marketer B's station will not necessarily consider Marketer A's station in Marketer B's price zone. This creates a series of overlapping but not coincident price zones that would allow price changes to affect neighboring zones. See also Maryland Energy Administration (2001).

[32] Without knowing the contours of a marketer's zones, we cannot quantify the degree of intra-brand, intra-zone price dispersion. However, we can look at intra-brand price dispersion within a fairly small geographic area. For example, in Arlington County, Virginia, for the fourth and fifth weeks of July 2001, five Texaco stations posted retail prices that differed substantially (see Table 1a) within each week. Even stations within two miles of one another (see Table 1b) posted prices that differed by five cents per gallon or more. Furthermore, looking across the two weeks one can see that these stations not only did not maintain a constant price differential from one another but also did not necessarily maintain the same rank.

[33] Of course, if retail markups differ within a price zone but remain constant over time, marketers could still monitor adherence to an agreement on DTW prices. However, in this case, the initial tacit collusion is much more complicated since the wholesale prices are not likely to be transparent to competing marketers. Furthermore, the marketers need to ensure that the markups remain constant for the tacit collusion to be successful. With variation in lessee markups, DTW prices are likely not transparent, making monitoring adherence to an agreement more difficult.

this way. Because price zones are not co-extensive across firms, punishing a price-cutter in one zone may create ripple effects in prices across neighboring zones. Thus, the response to a price-cutter may result in lower prices in multiple zones that then engender further price cuts, and so on. Rather than facilitating collusion, it seems just as likely that price zones may actually facilitate price wars.

Fourth, zone pricing likely makes reaching consensus more difficult. Economic theory suggests that coordinating firms typically want to *reduce* the number of prices or other dimensions on which they must coordinate, as coordination is more likely to be successful with a smaller number of things on which to agree and fewer dimensions on which firms must monitor adherence to an agreement. In the gasoline market, coordination on a single wholesale price – the rack price – would seem to be easier than coordination on an entire array of DTW prices.

Finally, for zone pricing to make coordination more effective, the conditions that make coordination feasible must be present. In particular, entry must be difficult. However, we see sections of the country where zone pricing has been employed, yet substantial entry has occurred. For example, Costco entered into gasoline retailing in San Diego in 1998 and expanded to seven locations in 2000.[34] The existence of such entry suggests that efforts to make coordination more effective or likely cannot explain the existence of zone pricing in these areas. This does not prove that zone pricing cannot be used to make coordination more effective in those areas where entry is difficult and the market structure is conducive to coordination; however, it does suggest that other reasons also explain the use of zone pricing and that a general ban on this practice could be harmful. Moreover, the foregoing arguments suggest that, as a

---

[34] Dan McSwain, "Gasoline's 'gouge gap' returns to North County," *North County Times*, Dec. 16, 2001. Available at http://www.nctimes.net/news/2001/20011216/55702.html. The article notes that Costco sells almost twice as much gasoline per station as ARCO, the market leader, and nearly four times as much as 76 (Tosco, now ConocoPhillips) stations.

general matter, zone pricing as it is currently employed does not appear to be a particularly good mechanism to facilitate coordination.

4.1.2 Entry Deterrence Theory

A second potential anticompetitive theory is that zone pricing allows marketers to make localized entry less profitable and thus more difficult by selectively lowering prices around the new entrant's station, thereby requiring an entrant to enter on a larger scale.[35] This theory assumes that marketers would not respond to larger-scale entry with similar (but broader-based) price cuts. If this behavior were unilateral, it is unlikely that one would be able to distinguish it for a normal competitive response to entry. If entry took place next to a company-owned station, a localized price response would be seen as entirely normal; the analysis should be no different because of the relationship between the lessee and the marketer. To look at the problem another way, suppose marketers were required to set a uniform price (net of delivery costs) to their lessee dealers. Entry would require the marketer to choose between maintaining its pre-entry wholesale price, thereby accepting a reduction in the margin that lessee dealers near the entrant earn, or cutting wholesale prices throughout the city in response to one new station.

The more likely of these outcomes, in our view, is that the marketer would maintain its pre-entry wholesale price. In fact, for an entry deterrence theory to be viable, the marketer under uniform pricing must either maintain its price or reduce price less. Otherwise, the ability to cut prices locally would have no impact on entry. Thus, the likely effect of requiring uniform

---

[35] See Vigdor (2003): "[Z]one pricing contributed to entry barriers by increasing the minimum efficient scale necessary to enter a market….[O]il companies create price zones around a new entrant and cut prices in those zones. Such price-cutting deters entry by increasing the minimum efficient scale necessary to enter a region. For example, the new entrant's profit margins and overall profits fall when competitors cut prices near the newly built retail outlet. That means new entrants will have to open more retail outlets and find larger quantities of gasoline to enter the area profitably." (pp. 12-13) Zone pricing creates "an additional entry barrier – a reputation effect. That is, new entrants learn that post-entry prices and profits will be low and therefore choose not to enter a market where oil companies use zone pricing." (p. 13)

pricing is that while entry might be more profitable and thus more likely to occur (although this is uncertain), the reaction to entry by incumbents will be less strong. Thus, the immediate benefits to consumers of lower market prices from entry will be reduced. This harm to consumers would then have to be compared to the potential benefit to consumers of possible increased competition more generally at some time in the future. To this extent, concerns about zone pricing as an entry deterrence mechanism are very similar to price predation concerns. As with price predation, it is very important not to confuse normal competitive responses with anticompetitive behavior.

The impact of requiring uniform prices may also have other, longer-run competitive implications. Ultimately, in a competitive market for lessee dealers, the dealer that faces new entry will be unable to earn a normal rate of return on that location and the incumbent (or the entrant) will exit or switch brands.[36] If one of the dealers exits, consumers are clearly worse off than they would be if the marketer were allowed to offer a localized wholesale price cut.

Furthermore, even if the marketer does lower wholesale prices to all lessee dealers following competitive entry at one location, it is likely that most of this benefit of lower wholesale prices to distant retailers would go to the lessee dealer in the form of higher profits rather than to consumers at those stations in the form of lower retail prices. Thus, the result to consumers may be little different than with zone pricing. In areas where new entry has occurred, consumers will get lower prices as would occur under zone pricing (although these prices might be higher if the uniform wholesale price decrease is smaller than would occur under zone

---

[36] This assumes that the rent the marketer charges the dealer remains constant. An alternative possibility is that the marketer could lower the rent; this is most likely to occur when the value of the land as a gas station exceeds the value for any alternative use. Even in this situation, however, the principal effect of banning price zones is to shift some economic quasi-rents from the marketer to the dealer. As we discuss in Section 4.2, this does not necessarily benefit consumers.

pricing) and this response would lower the profitability of entry. In areas where new entry has not occurred, consumers may see little price change as the dealers capture most of the rents from lower prices.[37]

Another problem with the theory that price zones are used to deter entry is that there has been substantial entry in many areas of the country. Even in southern California, where price zones have been well-documented, Costco has been able to enter and grow. A theory that price zones are used to deter entry would have to explain how significant entry can occur in the presence of price zones. For example, one might suggest that price zones are used to reduce the profitability of entry in markets with high concentration but not in markets with low concentration. We are unaware of any study of price zones that takes into account such differences across markets in a systematic manner.[38]

It is important to note that the use of price zones and other restrictions on gasoline retailers is a form of partial vertical integration. As the economics literature has shown, vertical integration raises anticompetitive concerns only if there exists market power upstream,

---

[37] It is possible that cutting prices in some areas could deter entry if the incumbent quickly gains a credible reputation for responding in such a way that entry will be unprofitable (Kreps and Wilson, 1982). Unless the incumbent has enough stations to compete with the entrant regardless of where the entrant locates, the entrant could avoid locating near an aggressive incumbent, and such a strategy would fail. Alternatively, if branded marketers face substantial economies of scope, thereby requiring that entry take place across multiple price zones, aggressive pricing in some zones could render entry unprofitable. However, the small scale of some successful entry suggests that scope economies are not so great in gasoline marketing as to preclude small-scale entry. For example, New Image Marketing data for 1999 from four counties in Northern Virginia show numerous market participants with a small number of stations, including chains such as Racetrac (2 stations), Coastal and Sheetz (4 each), BP and Getty (5 each), Hess (8), Chevron (11), Sunoco (15), and Crown (16). These firms all have market shares (as measured by station count) below 4%.

[38] Any such study would also have to control for factors *other* than price zones that increase retail prices. Leffler and Pulliam (1999) ascribe California's higher gasoline prices, in part, to price zones. However, Taylor and Fischer (2003) argue that gasoline prices are not higher in California than in Houston once taxes, higher production costs, and other factors are accounted for. Thus, an anticompetitive theory of price zones is not required to explain California retail pricing.

22

downstream, or at both levels.[39] The franchise literature (Klein and Saft (1985), Mathewson and Winter (1985)) shows that these types of restrictions are common and, more importantly, are not the result of franchisor market power. The fact that gasoline marketers with small market shares use these restrictions[40] also suggests that the profitability of the restrictions is not related to market power, and thus explanations unrelated to market power must explain at least some percentage (if not all) of these practices.

4.2 Business Justifications for Price Zones

Economic analysis suggests several business justifications for the use of price zones. This section discusses these reasons. We note upfront that, while these justifications appear plausible, we have limited evidence as to their validity. At best, we can observe that the reasons are consistent with the evidence. For example, the presence of zone pricing in areas where anticompetitive harm is unlikely because the market is relatively unconcentrated suggests that some or all justifications help explain the existence of zone pricing.

As a starting point, we first discuss why DTW prices might differ from rack plus transportation costs. While this in itself does not explain the existence of price zones, it helps to explain differential pricing between direct supplied and jobber supplied outlets. First, the marketer is providing much more than gasoline to its lessee dealers. The packages of goods and services that are provided to lessee dealers and to jobbers are very different. The marketer chooses the site and builds the station for its lessee dealers,[41] but jobber-supplied stations are

---

[39] Viscusi *et al.* (1992), p. 224.

[40] The Levin report on how gasoline prices are determined implies that all of the major marketers use zone pricing, and that the Washington, DC/Northern Virginia area is one area where the practice is common. Levin Hearings, pp. 642-46. As footnote 37 noted, several major marketers, including BP, Chevron, Sunoco, and Hess have market shares in Northern Virginia under 4%.

[41] As the owner of the site, the marketer also takes on the environmental risks of the station.

built by the local station owner (possibly the jobber itself) and the jobber is responsible for choosing which sites it will supply with branded gasoline. Because the marketer provides more services to the lessee dealer, the marketer will expect to be compensated for those services. One way that the marketer can be compensated is through a premium on wholesale gasoline prices. Part of the difference in wholesale prices between jobbers and lessee dealers may also be caused by discounts to jobbers. The marketer may give jobbers discounts on the wholesale price to give them an extra incentive to sell its brand of gasoline, through either new or existing stations.[42]

Second, DTW prices may exceed rack prices plus delivery costs due to dealers' risk-aversion. Dealers face at least two types of risk: supply disruptions and demand uncertainty. With regard to the first type, Marvel (2003) notes that a principal advantage to a dealer of establishing and maintaining a relationship with a branded marketer is that the marketer will supply branded dealers before unbranded dealers in the event of a supply disruption. The price of this supply "insurance" would be that DTW prices are above the rack price plus delivery costs on average. During periods of supply disruption, branded dealers benefit from this relationship; during normal times, branded dealers would prefer to purchase gasoline from the rack at a lower delivered cost. With regard to the second type of risk, the dealer may be willing to accept a lower average payout (including both the lease payment and retail gasoline margin) in exchange for more stable profits. If the marketer attempted to take all the expected profits as rent, relatively small reductions in the quantity demanded at that station may cause the dealer to lose money. The marketer can then increase its expected profits by reducing the dealer's risk by reducing the monthly rent and increasing the DTW price.

---

[42] In contrast to lessee dealers, jobbers often sell multiple brands of gasoline. As a result, jobbers may require additional incentives to sell a particular brand of gasoline.

We now turn to potential reasons for differential pricing across zones. First, one would expect any locational rents to accrue to the owner of the land.[43] For lessee dealers, the owner of the land is the marketer, but for jobber-supplied stations the owner of the land is usually the open dealer or the jobber. If the marketer cannot extract all of the locational rents from the fixed lease payment, then the marketer may charge higher DTW prices.[44] For example, marketers may face either practical or legal limits on how rapidly they can increase lease terms. This may have a substantial effect on the DTW price when the value of a site for use as a gasoline station is substantial. For example, if a city has very strict zoning regulations for gasoline stations but not other commercial real estate, the value of the gasoline station may be much higher than the underlying value of the land's next best (non-gasoline retail) alternative, such as a video rental store.

Furthermore, the marketer may want to reduce the lease payment and increase the DTW price to align the interests of the marketer and dealer. If the dealer contract provides for a monthly rent that reflects the full value of the station's location but a DTW price close to the marketer's cost, the lessee dealer has an incentive to exert more effort to sell more gasoline; conversely, if the dealer contract provides for a below-market monthly rent in return for a higher DTW price, the marketer has an incentive to work to help the lessee dealer sell more gasoline. In other words, having a higher DTW price and lower monthly rent helps to align the marketer's incentives with those of the dealer so that the marketer does not have an incentive just to take the monthly rent and let the dealer flounder in bad times. The optimal contract will likely reflect

---

[43] Lessee dealers argue that any locational rents at a site are due to the quality of the services that the dealer provides rather than the physical location, and therefore the lessee dealer is entitled to these rents. However, lessee dealer complaints on price zones may also involve lessee dealer and marketer disputes over how to split the profits of a station.

[44] Keeley and Elzinga (2003) make this argument as well.

involve something between the two extremes, with a monthly rent below the full market value of the property but above zero (i.e., with the DTW price capturing the entire value of the property). To the extent that the optimal tradeoff between lease payments and DTW prices various across an area, the marketer will find it profitable to employ station-specific pricing, or to group similar stations into zones.[45]

Finally, localized price zones give marketers the ability to react quickly to changes in the competitive environment, in a sense allowing the marketer to update a lessee dealer's rent on a daily basis. Therefore, if the Sam's Club down the road from a lessee dealer puts in gasoline pumps and begins to undercut the branded station, the marketer can quickly lower DTW prices to that station, allowing it to remain competitive. If the marketer instead charged a high lease rate and charged marginal cost for gasoline, the lessee dealer would end up no longer being able to make the lease payments on the station with the new, lower margins.[46] The marketer could attempt to lower the lease payments, but this would be much more costly than adjusting the wholesale price, and may take too long to be useful to the lessee dealer. As with the previous point about the optimal split between DTW price and monthly rent, price zones (or, in the limit, station-specific pricing) are used to confine the changes to the affected areas.

These reasons for using zone pricing, if correct, benefit consumers, both directly and indirectly. Enforcing uniform wholesale prices throughout a delivery area (excluding delivery costs) would result in some wholesale prices that are "too high" and some that are "too low."

---

[45] For example, concerns that the marketer treat similar stations similarly under the Robinson-Patman Act may lead to the use of common DTW pricing for nearby stations. See Vigdor (2003).

[46] Similarly, if a new outlet mall opens across the street from a lessee dealer that previously had low traffic volumes, without zone pricing, the lessee dealer would capture all the benefits from the new traffic as retail prices increased. With price zones, the marketer, who took the risk in investing in the station in the first place, is able to increase wholesale prices and capture most of the gain from the improved location. Eventually, the marketer could have increased the lease payments, but that would likely take much longer to implement, and may transfer too much risk to the lessee dealer.

Consumers in areas with high wholesale prices under uniform pricing clearly benefit from zone pricing; consumers in areas with low wholesale prices under uniform pricing do not necessarily benefit much from this situation, because dealers will capture most of the gain. Zone pricing also may benefit consumers indirectly in two ways. First, to the extent that zone pricing allows for a better alignment of risk between the branded marketer and the dealer, prices will be lower, all else equal. Second, to the extent that zone pricing allows branded marketers to capture the value of their investments in land and stations, marketers will make the optimal level of investments. The alternative would seem to be more widespread use of open dealers who then affiliate with branded marketers. However, dealers tend to be small businessmen, less able to withstand the ups and downs of the business than the large branded marketers, and dealers may have less expertise in choosing optimal sites.

5   Redlining

As noted in Section 2, the term "redlining" is used to refer to restrictions on jobbers' supplying specific stations in areas with direct distribution and to restrictions on a jobber's ability to arbitrage from low-priced zones to high-priced zones. This section explores possible anticompetitive theories and procompetitive rationales for redlining.

5.1 Anticompetitive Theories of Redlining

Opponents of redlining have suggested three possible competitive concerns with the practice. The principal concern appears to be that the practice reduces intra-brand competition in a way that engenders higher retail prices. Second, the presence of redlining has been used as an argument that a market may not be fully competitive, thereby justifying more aggressive antitrust intervention than otherwise. Finally, redlining may be necessary to support price zones, so that if price zones raise competitive issues, redlining may as well.

Much of the criticism against redlining and, indirectly, price zones is focused on the role of intra-brand competition in maintaining competitive retail gasoline prices. For example, the Petroleum Marketers Association of America (2003) claims that, "By limiting intra-brand competition…refiners [branded marketers] are afforded a monopoly on the brand and, as a consequence, brand-loyal customers are reduced to a single purchase option….In dual distribution areas…, where intra-brand competition is allowed to flourish, consumers generally enjoy the benefit of lower prices."[47] To the extent that redlining is analogous to other non-price vertical restraints, the empirical literature discussed in Section 3 does not support this proposition, nor does the experimental work of Deck and Wilson (2003).

More generally, exclusive territories are typically examined under the rule of reason. This is because exclusive territories, like other non-price vertical restraints, have procompetitive explanations, involving the provision of correct incentives to dealers.[48] Although such restraints also have the potential to be used to enhance the likelihood or stability of coordination,[49] one would not want to impose on marketers an obligation to create intra-brand competition without solid evidence that restricting intra-brand competition significantly enhances coordination.

---

[47] The Petroleum Marketers Association of America, despite the name, is a group affiliated with gasoline jobbers and dealers, not marketers. Kleit (2003, p. 28) observes that the interests of complaining dealers are not necessarily those of consumers.

[48] Boyd (1993). Boyd argues that firms with long product life cycles are more likely to use exclusive territories, whereas firms with shorter product life cycles are more likely to use resale price maintenance to protect dealer services.

[49] Rey and Stiglitz (1995) argue that territorial restraints can decrease the demand elasticity that producers face, which reduces inter-brand competition.

How would redlining help prevent inter-brand coordination among marketers from breaking down through intra-brand competition? Suppose marketers have found a way to coordinate prices within a price zone. Clearly, arbitrage by jobbers – transporting gasoline from low-priced zones to high-priced zones whenever the difference in the transportation cost is sufficiently small that the jobber can profitably undercut the DTW price – would undermine this coordination, unless all jobbers were part of the scheme. Furthermore, allowing jobbers to supply stations within the area of coordination, whether through conversion of existing stations from one brand to another or through construction of new, jobber-owned stations, and to supply those stations at the competitive rack price plus a cost-based delivery charge, would undermine the coordination.

Although this theory is internally consistent, there are a number of reasons to question its empirical relevance. First, the theory assumes that marketers can coordinate prices. As discussed in Section 4, coordination on different prices in different zones does not appear likely because coordination would be more difficult as the number of prices on which to coordinate increases.[50]

In addition, successful coordination requires that sufficient entry by other marketers is unlikely. Entry by marketers may not be unlikely, at least in some areas. In order to defeat a coordinated price increase in any particular zone, it may not be necessary to have *de novo* entry into a broad geographic area. This would be the case if marketers that are not already participating in that zone but are present in nearby zones.[51] Also, in many parts of the country, it

---

[50] In principle, it could be the case that each price zone is effectively its own geographic market. In that case, coordination might be possible in some zones but not others, and redlining would prevent arbitrage across markets. If this were the case, however, one would expect to see price zones that were similar across firms. As the Commission noted in the Western States investigation, this does not appear to be the case. (Western States Gasoline Statement.)

[51] For example, a marketer may have branded stations in Northern Virginia (served by a terminal in Fairfax) but not in the Maryland suburbs of Washington, DC (also served by the Fairfax terminal). If prices in a suburban Maryland

may not be necessary for an entrant to have a major brand. Entry could be by a hypermarket, such as Costco and Wal-Mart,[52] by a low-price, high-volume brand, such as Sheetz or Racetrac, or by other unbranded stations.[53] Even though entry by hypermarkets often involves unbranded gasoline, the substantial sales that hypermarkets enjoy in some areas suggests that they can be an important competitive constraint on major brands.

The second concern about redlining is the belief that a marketer's ability to use redlining implies that the market is not competitive.[54] However, as we explained above in connection with zone pricing, the ability of a firm to engage in price discrimination across geographic areas is not a good indication of substantial market power.[55] Furthermore, it seems inappropriate to focus concern over this practice on gasoline retailing. Firms limit intra-brand competition in other markets. For example, franchisors frequently limit how close to an existing franchise a new

---

price zone were to increase as the result of coordination among existing marketers, expansion by marketers now serving Virginia only may now become profitable.

[52] Hypermarkets "can typically establish a significant market presence in a relatively short time. They tend to use very competitive gasoline pricing to build traffic on their site. The increased traffic, in turn, generates incremental store sales with margins much higher than those on gasoline." J.S. Carter (ExxonMobil) statement, Levin Hearings, pp. 133-34.

[53] In other areas, such as California, having a major brand may be important for reasons unrelated to redlining. During supply disruptions, unbranded gasoline becomes extremely scarce as the branded marketers attempt to make sure their stations are supplied. These supply disruptions occasionally result in price inversions, where unbranded gasoline becomes more expensive than branded gasoline at the wholesale rack. These price inversions have driven most independents to affiliate with one of the marketers, or exit the market all together. Therefore, the scarce resource that the jobber needs to open a station is someone to commit to supply him gasoline during supply disruptions at prices comparable to the branded marketers. If a marketer is reluctant to commit to supply gasoline to new branded stations during what appear to be inevitable price spikes on the West Coast, the marketer may use redlining to force the jobber to find sites in areas where the marketer does not already have a network of stations. In this case it is the assured supply rather than the brand that is important, and one of the reasons that most of California's unbranded gasoline stations have exited or affiliated with branded marketers.

[54] For example, see Petroleum Marketers Association of America (2003).

[55] Klein and Wiley (2003); Baumol and Swanson (2003). Keeley and Elzinga (2003) argue that price differences across price zones are unlikely to be economic price discrimination, as price discrimination is difficult to sustain in the long run in a competitive market. Of course, whether these markets are, in fact, workably competitive is precisely the question at hand.

franchise may locate. Firms also frequently employ exclusive territories for sales representatives.[56]

The third concern is that, by preventing arbitrage, redlining helps to maintain price zones in two ways. First, redlining could prevent jobbers who pay a lower rack price from supplying lessee dealers that the marketer supplies at higher DTW prices. Second, redlining could prevent jobbers from opening new branded stations in what are currently high price zones for that brand. However, redlining does not appear to be necessary to prevent lessee dealers from engaging in arbitrage because a marketer, though contract terms with its lessees, can require that its lessee dealers purchase gasoline from the marketer alone. In addition, even if redlining prevents jobbers from undermining the local DTW price for a particular brand, redlining does not prevent unbranded entry or entry of other brands.[57] In theory, marketers could collude to impose redlining restrictions in order to deter entry, but the Commission has not alleged that redlining is the result of coordinated behavior among marketers.

5.2 Business Justifications for Redlining

Marketers can be expected to choose different methods of distribution according to specific market needs. Where one brand has a limited presence, it is often efficient for the marketer to use jobber distribution to economize on distribution costs, as the jobber can supply stations of multiple brands. In addition, jobbers may have better information than the marketer about new opportunities for station locations. Where a brand has a greater presence, direct

---

[56] Mathewson and Winter (1994) find territorial restrictions in half of their sample of 24 franchise contracts, including fast food (Arby's, Chicken Delight, Hardee's, Long John Silver, and Swiss Chalet), computers (Computerland, Entre Computer, Micro Age, Software Centre), video rental (National Video), printing (PIP), and snowmobile sales (Bombardier). Jordan and Jaffee (1987) discuss exclusive territories in beer distribution.

[57] Although there are regions of the country, such as California, where entry is difficult because of difficulties in obtaining bulk gasoline supplies, and there are local areas in which government zoning regulations make entry difficult, these problems are unrelated to redlining.

distribution, whether through company-owned stations or lessee dealer stations, may be a more efficient arrangement. The marketer can eliminate the successive markups that a separate distribution system entails, along with any agency problems that arise with jobbers. Furthermore, different marketers have different business strategies for station ownership: some prefer to own stations outright, some prefer lessee dealers in order to mitigate agency problems, and some prefer to sign up open dealers in order to limit their own capital expenditures.

One possible reason for territorial restrictions on jobbers is to prevent inefficiencies from dual distribution.[58] Absent these restrictions, jobbers could cherry-pick good sites within the marketer's distribution system and deliver to those stations, increasing distribution costs for the marketer (Marvel (2003)). Dual distribution also could lead to inefficient duplication of assets by the marketer and jobber.

These territorial restrictions also prevent jobbers from free-riding on the investments that marketers make in building their networks of direct supply stations, because part of the return on investment is the profits from supplying wholesale gasoline to those sites (Kleit (2003)). With lessee dealers, as discussed in Section 4, marketers have an incentive to reduce the lease terms and increase the DTW price in order to shift risk from the dealer to the marketer and to create greater incentive compatibility between the marketer and its dealers. Redlining restrictions, to the extent they allow the marketer to maintain a DTW price, also permit the marketer to capture the return to the site. Allowing jobbers to sell to lessee dealers or to supply new open dealers at rack prices plus transportation cost would undermine these efforts. These issues do not arise, or arise

---

[58] Jobbers also seem to benefit from distribution restrictions. Marketers will often give jobbers exclusive territories where they will be the only jobber that can supply the marketer's brand of gasoline, or create new branded stations.

to a lesser degree, with open dealers, as their relationship to marketers involves a more arm's-length relationship.

Consumers benefit from these business motivations for redlining, albeit indirectly. First, any inefficiencies in dual distribution will lead to higher costs of supplying gasoline and, therefore, to higher prices. Second, allowing branded marketers to capture the return from their investments in land and stations results in the optimal level of investment and, therefore, greater retail competition than would otherwise exist.[59]

6   Conclusion

Concerns over price zones and redlining continue to draw public attention. However, these concerns are based on the assumption that the rack prices and non-price terms between marketers and dealers that exist today would continue in a world without price zones and/or redlining. To the extent that the DTW price reflects the provision of services to lessee dealers that jobbers provide to open dealers, or, to put it another way, that the rack price allows jobbers an additional margin for services they provide to open dealers, one would expect that banning these restraints would increase rack prices relative to DTW prices. Economic theory, empirical research, and experimental research all provide reasons to believe that banning price zones would be likely to result in higher average prices.

In some ways, complaints about redlining amount to arguments that franchisors – in this case, the marketers – should be prohibited from controlling the location of and terms of trade with their franchisees, either dealers or jobbers. Hovenkamp (2001, pp. 304-11) argues that attempts to turn franchise disputes into antitrust disputes are misguided. "[C]alling this kind of

---

[59] As the discussion of zone pricing indicated, there may be reasons why dealers or jobbers would not make those investments, or at least not to the same level as branded marketers, if redlining were banned.

control [the ability to raise the price of specified inputs] 'market power' is not merely legally incorrect, it is also extremely dangerous as a policy matter. It threatens to turn antitrust into an engine for the resolution of all kinds of disputes over long-term contracts, or worse yet, to use antitrust as a device for protecting people from their own careless bargaining." (p. 306)

As this paper has shown, both price zones and redlining have business explanations other than anticompetitive motivations. Price zones allow branded marketers who own gasoline stations to capture the returns from good locations – returns that would otherwise be captured by station lessees. Price zones may permit an efficient allocation of risk between the marketer and lessee dealer, and help align the incentives of the marketer and its lessee dealers. Redlining, by helping to maintain zone pricing, facilitates the procompetitive effects of zones. Redlining may also help maintain a more efficient delivery system by preventing jobbers from cherry-picking the most profitable stations to supply, thereby increasing economies of scale or scope in distribution and avoiding duplicative investments in distribution assets. These results are consistent with both economic theory and empirical work on vertical restraints in the gasoline industry.

One likely consequence of prohibiting contractual provisions such as zone pricing and redlining is that marketers will use other, less-efficient means of achieving the same goals. For example, marketers can increase the fraction of company-owned stations in areas without divorcement laws; if this were more efficient than using lessee dealers, presumably the marketers would have done so already. This suggests that regulators need to be careful to consider how firms will react to restrictions on their ability to operate their businesses.

As we noted in the introduction to this paper, determining whether a practice is anticompetitive requires a sound economic theory of harm and evidence consistent with the

34

theory. Conversely, one can infer the likely existence of procompetitive effects from conduct that occurs where anticompetitive effects appear unlikely. The existence of zone pricing and redlining in areas of the country where entry has occurred into gasoline marketing suggests that one or more of the business justifications, rather than the anticompetitive explanations, is likely to explain these practices in such areas. Thus, in parts of the country where entry may be impeded for one reason or another, where we cannot exclude the anticompetitive theories *a priori*, we cannot exclude the procompetitive justifications, either. As a consequence, antitrust policy should not condemn zone pricing or redlining across the board, nor conclude that the presence of the practices indicates the existence of market power, but should instead require market-specific evidence that the practices have resulted in higher retail gasoline prices.

References

Barron, John M. and John R. Umbeck, 1984. "The Effects of Different Contractual Arrangements: The Case of Retail Gasoline Markets," *Journal of Law and Economics,* vol. 27, pp. 313-28.

Baumol, William J. and Daniel G. Swanson, 2003. "The New Economy and Ubiquitous *Competitive* Price Discrimination: Identifying Defensible Criteria of Market Power," *Antitrust Law Journal,* vol. 70, pp. 661-85.

Blass, Asher A. and Dennis W. Carlton, 2001. "The Choice of Organizational Form in Gasoline Retailing and the Cost of Laws that Limit that Choice," *Journal of Law and Economics,* vol. 44, pp. 511-24.

Boyd, David W., 1993. "The Choice Between Resale Price Maintenance and Exclusive Territories: Evidence from Litigation," *Review of Industrial Organization*, vol. 8, pp. 755-63.

Comanor, William S. and Jon M. Riddle, 2003. "The Costs of Regulation: Branded Open Supply and Uniform Pricing of Gasoline," *International Journal of the Economics of Business,* vol. 10, pp. 135-55.

Deck, Cary A. and Bart J. Wilson, 2003. "Experimental Gasoline Markets," FTC Working Paper No. 263.

Dnes, Antony W., 1993. "A Case-Study Analysis of Franchise Contracts," *Journal of Legal Studies,* vol. 22, pp. 367-93.

Hastings, Justine, 2002. "Vertical Relationships and Competition in Retail Gasoline Markets," working paper.

Hastings, Justine and Richard Gilbert, 2002. "Market Power, Vertical Integration and the Wholesale Price of Gasoline," working paper.

Hovenkamp, Herbert, 2001. "Post-Chicago Antitrust: A Review and Critique," *2001 Columbia Business Law Review* pp. 257-337.

Jordan, W. John and Bruce L. Jaffee, 1987. "The Use of Exclusive Territories in the Distribution of Beer: Theoretical and Empirical Observations," *Antitrust Bulletin*, vol. 32, pp. 137-64.

Kaufmann, Patrick J. and Francine Lafontaine, 1994. "Costs of Control: The Source of Economic Rents for McDonald's Franchisees," *Journal of Law and Economics,* vol. 37, pp. 417-53.

Keeley, Michael C. and Kenneth G. Elzinga, 2003. "Uniform Gasoline Price Regulation: Consequences for Consumer Welfare," *International Journal of the Economics of Business,* vol.

10, pp. 157-68.

Klein, Benjamin and Lester F. Saft, 1985. "The Law and Economics of Franchise Tying Contracts," *Journal of Law and Economics,* vol. 28, pp. 345-61.

Klein, Benjamin and John Shepard Wiley, Jr., 2003. "Competitive Price Discrimination as an Antitrust Justification for Intellectual Property Refusals to Deal," *Antitrust Law Journal,* vol. 70, pp. 599-642.

Kleit, Andrew N., 2003. "The Economics of Gasoline Retailing: Petroleum Distribution and Retailing Issues in the U.S.," American Petroleum Institute, December.

Kreps, David and Robert Wilson, 1982. "Reputation and Imperfect Information," *Journal of Economic Theory*, vol. 27, pp. 253-79.

Leffler, Keith and Barry Pulliam, 1999. "Preliminary Report to the Attorney General Regarding California Gasoline Prices," manuscript.

Marvel, Howard P., 2003. "On the Economics of Branded Open Supply," *International Journal of the Economics of Business,* vol. 10, pp. 213-23.

Maryland Energy Administration, 2001. "Task Force Report on Gasoline Zone Pricing," Sept. 14, 2001. Available from the Maryland Energy Administration.

Mathewson, G. Frank and Ralph A. Winter, 1985. "The Economics of Franchise Contracts," *Journal of Law and Economics,* vol. 28, pp. 503-26.

Mathewson, Frank and Ralph Winter, 1994. "Territorial Restrictions in Franchise Contracts," *Economic Inquiry*, vol. 32, pp. 181-92.

O'Brien, Daniel P. and Greg Shaffer, 1994. "The Welfare Effects of Forbidding Discriminatory Discounts: A Secondary Line Analysis of Robinson-Patman," *Journal of Law, Economics, and Organization,* vol. 10, pp. 296-318.

Petroleum Marketers Association of America, 2003. "PMAA White Paper on Refiner Redlining in Historic Independent Marketer Territories."

Rey, Patrick and Joseph Stiglitz, 1995. "The Role of Exclusive Territories in Producers' Competition," *RAND Journal of Economics*, vol. 26, pp. 431-51.

Shepard, Andrea, 1993. "Contractual Form, Retail Price, and Asset Characteristics in Gasoline Retailing," *RAND Journal of Economics,* vol. 24, pp. 58-77.

Taylor, Beck A., 2000. "Retail Characteristics and Ownership Structure," *Small Business Economics,* vol. 12, pp. 157-64.

Taylor, Christopher T. and Jeffrey H. Fischer, 2003. "A Review of West Coast Gasoline Pricing and the Impact of Regulations," *International Journal of the Economics of Business,* vol. 10, pp. 225-43.

Tirole, Jean, 1997. *The Theory of Industrial Organization,* Ninth printing. The MIT Press.

Vigdor, William R., 2003. "Antitrust Treatment of Zone Pricing and Redlining," ABA Section of Law Course Materials, April 2, 2003. Available upon request from Vinson & Elkins, LLP.

Viscusi, W. Kip, John M. Vernon, and Joseph E. Harrington, Jr., 1992. *Economics of Regulation and Antitrust.* D.C. Heath and Co.

Vita, Michael G., 2000. "Regulatory Restrictions on Vertical Integration and Control: The Competitive Impact of Gasoline Divorcement Policies," *Journal of Regulatory Economics*, vol. 18, pp. 217-33.

Table 1a: Arlington Co., Virginia Texaco prices for two weeks in July 2001

	Week of 7/22/01	Week of 7/29/01
Clarendon Gas & Co./Texaco	$1.53	$1.52
Columbia Pike Texaco	$1.58	$1.60
Shirlington Texaco	$1.63	$1.59
Texaco D&V Auto Service Center	$1.55	$1.53
Texaco Food Mart	$1.50	$1.46

Source: OPIS. Prices are for regular unleaded gasoline.

Table 1b: Distance Between Arlington Co., Virginia Texaco Stations

	Clarendon	Columbia Pk.	Shirlington	D & V Auto	Food Mart
Clarendon	---	1.95	3.78	3.39	2.09
Columbia Pike		---	2.70	4.70	3.00
Shirlington			---	7.34	4.06
D & V Auto				---	1.77
Food Mart					---

Source: Mapblast (www.mapblast.com). Distance in miles.